Sinatra Standards

FOR PIANISTS

I've Got You Under My
It Might As Well Be S
Come Rain Or Come Shine
Witchcraft
Young At Heart
It's All Right With Me
This is All I Ask
The Best Is Yet To Come
All The Way
Teach Me Tonight

3069

MUSIC MINUS ONE 50 Executive Boulevard • Elmsford New York 10523-1325

2

Printed in Canada

Music Minus One

MMO CD 3069

Sinatra Standards Set To Music

I've Got You Under My Skin

Words and Music by Cole Porter

A repeating swinging band figure immediately sets the mood. Since the background at the chorus is busy, piano starts with melody in octaves, and then goes on to utilise other textures with a change in register. I then proceed to use more elaborations, fill-ins, and improvisations around melody. At the bridge, the piano is obliged to respect and fit in with the rhythmic band figures. It is only after this ceases that I am freed to improvise freely. Notice how the improvisation tries to preserve the contours of melody, improvising "around the melody," so to speak. This is a useful device to cultivate. After a long rhythmic band interlude followed by an exciting ensemble section, the piano returns with a very simple treatment of melody to both contrast with the preceding excitement and to avoi clashing with the underlying busy background figures. At the very end, I remind the listener that the piano is still very much alive by punching out the final chord with the band.

6

It Might As Well Be Spring

Words and Music by Richard Rodgers and Oscar Hammerstein III

After a beautifully lush short orchestral introduction, the piano continues the established mood with melody in a variety of textures. The background, as always, dictates what we should play as we strive for total sonic clarity. Since the bridge permits freer playing, I respond with a more elaborate improvisation that continues into the next phrase with a still freer approach, but then return to melody at an appropriate point. Notice how, near the end of this piece, the piano carefully follows the irregular slow pace of the orchestra with improvised arpeggiated figures designed to gracefully maintain the piano's involvement as a cooperative contributor to the end.

12

Come Rain Or Come Shine

Words by Johnny Mercer
Music by Harold Arlen

14

This begins with a very attractive intro by muted trumpet with orchestra. Piano enters with pianistic figurations elaborating the melody as it follows the free-tempo pace of the orchestra. When the rhythm section enters to establish tempo, the piano continues in similar fashion. Notice how I try to constantly respond to opportunites to improvise, but then return to melody when this seems appropriate. Since music unfolds in time, we must be prepared to quickly respond to ever-changing moods as a piece proceeds and develops. J. O.

16

18

20

Witchcraft

After a rhythmic band intro, piano enters at the chorus with full voicings, melody in octaves, lower-register octaves, and improvisation. An ascending scale leads to melody at the bridge, followed by playful, free improvisation based on chords. The last phrase features block-chord improvisation followed by melody in octaves in the piano's lower register. The band then plays an ensemble section as piano fills in the empty spaces. In the middle of the next bridge section, the piano appropriately engages once again in playful improvisation. The final phrase features melody played with three rapid changes of texture, after which the piano punches out the final chord with the band. J. O.

Music by Cy Coleman
Lyric by Carolyn Leigh

21

And I've got no de-fense for it, the heat is too in-tense for it, what good would com-mon sense for it do? 'Cause it's witch - craft Wick - ed witch - craft though I know it's strict - ly ta - boo

22

24

MMO Compact Disc Catalog

BROADWAY

_____ LES MISERABLES/PHANTOM OF THE OPERA	MMO CD 1016
_____ HITS OF ANDREW LLOYD WEBBER	MMO CD 1054
_____ GUYS AND DOLLS	MMO CD 1067
_____ WEST SIDE STORY 2 CD Set	MMO CD 1100
_____ CABARET 2 CD Set	MMO CD 1110
_____ BROADWAY HEROES AND HEROINES	MMO CD 1121
_____ CAMELOT	MMO CD 1173
_____ BEST OF ANDREW LLOYD WEBBER	MMO CD 1130
_____ THE SOUND OF BROADWAY	MMO CD 1133
_____ BROADWAY MELODIES	MMO CD 1134
_____ BARBRA'S BROADWAY	MMO CD 1144
_____ JEKYLL & HYDE	MMO CD 1151
_____ SHOWBOAT	MMO CD 1160
_____ MY FAIR LADY 2 CD Set	MMO CD 1174
_____ OKLAHOMA	MMO CD 1175
_____ THE SOUND OF MUSIC 2 CD Set	MMO CD 1176
_____ SOUTH PACIFIC	MMO CD 1177
_____ THE KING AND I	MMO CD 1178
_____ FIDDLER ON THE ROOF 2 CD Set	MMO CD 1179
_____ CAROUSEL	MMO CD 1180
_____ PORGY AND BESS	MMO CD 1181
_____ THE MUSIC MAN	MMO CD 1183
_____ ANNIE GET YOUR GUN 2 CD Set	MMO CD 1186
_____ HELLO DOLLY! 2 CD Set	MMO CD 1187
_____ OLIVER 2 CD Set	MMO CD 1189
_____ SUNSET BOULEVARD	MMO CD 1193
_____ GREASE	MMO CD 1196
_____ SMOKEY JOE'S CAFE	MMO CD 1197
_____ MISS SAIGON	MMO CD 1226

CLARINET

_____ MOZART CONCERTO, IN A, K.622	MMO CD 3201
_____ WEBER CONCERTO NO. 1 in Fm. STAMITZ CONC. No. 3 IN Bb	MMO CD 3202
_____ SPOHR CONCERTO NO. 1 in C MINOR OP. 26	MMO CD 3203
_____ WEBER CONCERTO OP. 26, BEETHOVEN TRIO OP. 11	MMO CD 3204
_____ FIRST CHAIR CLARINET SOLOS	MMO CD 3205
_____ THE ART OF THE SOLO CLARINET:	MMO CD 3206
_____ MOZART QUINTET IN A, K.581	MMO CD 3207
_____ BRAHMS SONATAS OP. 120 NO. 1 & 2	MMO CD 3208
_____ WEBER GRAND DUO CONCERTANT WAGNER ADAGIO	MMO CD 3209
_____ SCHUMANN FANTASY OP. 73, 3 ROMANCES OP. 94	MMO CD 3210
_____ EASY CLARINET SOLOS Volume 1 - STUDENT LEVEL	MMO CD 3211
_____ EASY CLARINET SOLOS Volume 2 - STUDENT LEVEL	MMO CD 3212
_____ EASY JAZZ DUETS - STUDENT LEVEL	MMO CD 3213
_____ VISIONS The Clarinet Artistry of Ron Odrich	MMO CD 3214
_____ IN A LEAGUE OF HIS OWN Popular Songs played by Ron Odrich and You	MMO CD 3215
_____ SINATRA SET TO MUSIC Kern, Weill, Gershwin, Howard and You	MMO CD 3216
_____ STRAVINSKY: L'HISTOIRE DU SOLDAT	MMO CD 3217
_____ ECLECTIC CLARINET Larry Linkon (2 CD Set)	MMO CD 3218
_____ JAZZ STANDARDS WITH STRINGS FOR CLARINET (2 CD Set)	MMO CD 3219
_____ RON ODRICH PLAYS STANDARDS	MMO CD 3220
_____ BEGINNING CONTEST SOLOS - Jerome Bunke, Clinician	MMO CD 3221
_____ BEGINNING CONTEST SOLOS - Harold Wright	MMO CD 3222
_____ INTERMEDIATE CONTEST SOLOS - Stanley Drucker	MMO CD 3223
_____ INTERMEDIATE CONTEST SOLOS - Jerome Bunke, Clinician	MMO CD 3224
_____ ADVANCED CONTEST SOLOS - Stanley Drucker	MMO CD 3225
_____ ADVANCED CONTEST SOLOS - Harold Wright	MMO CD 3226
_____ INTERMEDIATE CONTEST SOLOS - Stanley Drucker	MMO CD 3227
_____ ADVANCED CONTEST SOLOS - Stanley Drucker	MMO CD 3228
_____ ADVANCED CONTEST SOLOS - Harold Wright	MMO CD 3229
_____ BRAHMS Clarinet Quintet in Bm, Op. 115	MMO CD 3230
_____ TEACHER'S PARTNER Basic Clarinet Studies	MMO CD 3231
_____ JEWELS FOR WOODWIND QUINTET	MMO CD 3232
_____ WOODWIND QUINTETS minus CLARINET	MMO CD 3233
_____ FROM DIXIE to SWING	MMO CD 3234
_____ BEETHOVEN: QUINTET FOR CLARINET in Eb Major, Opus 16	MMO CD 3235
_____ MOZART: QUINTET FOR CLARINET in Eb. K.452	MMO CD 3236
_____ THE VIRTUOSO CLARINETIST Baermann Method, Op. 63 4 CD Set	MMO CD 3240
_____ ART OF THE CLARINET Baermann Method, Op. 64 4 CD Set	MMO CD 3241
_____ POPULAR CONCERT FAVORITES WITH ORCHESTRA	MMO CD 3242
_____ BAND-AIDS CONCERT BAND FAVORITES WITH ORCHESTRA	MMO CD 3243
_____ WORLD FAVORITES Student Editions, 41 Easy Selections (1st-2nd year)	MMO CD 3244
_____ CLASSIC THEMES Student Editions, 27 Easy Songs (2nd-3rd year)	MMO CD 3245

PIANO

_____ BEETHOVEN CONCERTO NO. 1 IN C	MMO CD 3001
_____ BEETHOVEN CONCERTO NO. 2 IN Bb	MMO CD 3002
_____ BEETHOVEN CONCERTO NO. 3 IN C MINOR	MMO CD 3003
_____ BEETHOVEN CONCERTO NO. 4 IN G	MMO CD 3004
_____ BEETHOVEN CONCERTO NO. 5 IN Eb (2 CD SET)	MMO CD 3005
_____ GRIEG CONCERTO IN A MINOR OP.16	MMO CD 3006
_____ RACHMANINOFF CONCERTO NO. 2 IN C MINOR	MMO CD 3007
_____ SCHUMANN CONCERTO IN A MINOR	MMO CD 3008
_____ BRAHMS CONCERTO NO. 1 IN D MINOR (2 CD SET)	MMO CD 3009
_____ CHOPIN CONCERTO NO. 1 IN E MINOR OP. 11	MMO CD 3010
_____ MENDELSSOHN CONCERTO NO. 1 IN G MINOR	MMO CD 3011
_____ MOZART CONCERTO NO. 9 IN Eb K.271	MMO CD 3012
_____ MOZART CONCERTO NO. 12 IN A K.414	MMO CD 3013
_____ MOZART CONCERTO NO. 20 IN D MINOR K.466	MMO CD 3014
_____ MOZART CONCERTO NO. 23 IN A K.488	MMO CD 3015
_____ MOZART CONCERTO NO. 24 IN C MINOR K.491	MMO CD 3016
_____ MOZART CONCERTO NO. 26 IN D K.537, CORONATION	MMO CD 3017
_____ MOZART CONCERTO NO. 17 IN G K.453	MMO CD 3018
_____ LISZT CONCERTO NO. 1 IN Eb, WEBER OP. 79	MMO CD 3019
_____ LISZT CONCERTO NO. 2 IN A, HUNGARIAN FANTASIA	MMO CD 3020
_____ J.S. BACH CONCERTO IN F MINOR, J.C. BACH CON. IN Eb	MMO CD 3021
_____ J.S. BACH CONCERTO IN D MINOR	MMO CD 3022
_____ HAYDN CONCERTO IN D	MMO CD 3023
_____ HEART OF THE PIANO CONCERTO	MMO CD 3024
_____ THEMES FROM GREAT PIANO CONCERTI	MMO CD 3025
_____ TSCHAIKOVSKY CONCERTO NO. 1 IN Bb MINOR	MMO CD 3026
_____ ART OF POPULAR PIANO PLAYING, Vol. 1 STUDENT LEVEL	MMO CD 3033
_____ ART OF POPULAR PIANO PLAYING, Vol. 2 STUDENT LEVEL 2 CD Set	MMO CD 3034
_____ 'POP' PIANO FOR STARTERS STUDENT LEVEL	MMO CD 3035
_____ DVORAK TRIO IN A MAJOR, OP. 90 "Dumky Trio"	MMO CD 3037
_____ DVORAK QUINTET IN A MAJOR, OP. 81	MMO CD 3038
_____ MENDELSSOHN TRIO IN D MAJOR, OP. 49	MMO CD 3039
_____ MENDELSSOHN TRIO IN C MINOR, OP. 66	MMO CD 3040
_____ BLUES FUSION FOR PIANO	MMO CD 3049
_____ CLAUDE BOLLING SONATA FOR FLUTE AND JAZZ PIANO TRIO	MMO CD 3050
_____ TWENTY DIXIELAND CLASSICS	MMO CD 3051
_____ TWENTY RHYTHM BACKGROUNDS TO STANDARDS	MMO CD 3052
_____ FROM DIXIE to SWING	MMO CD 3053
_____ J.S. BACH BRANDENBURG CONCERTO NO. 5 IN D MAJOR	MMO CD 3054
_____ BACH Cm CONC. - 2 PIANOS / SCHUMANN & VAR., OP. 46 - 2 PIANOS	MMO CD 3055
_____ J.C. BACH Bm CONC./HAYDN C CONCERT./HANDEL CONC. GROSSO-D	MMO CD 3056
_____ J.S. BACH TRIPLE CONCERTO IN A MINOR	MMO CD 3057
_____ FRANCK SYM. VAR. / MENDELSSOHN: CAPRICCO BRILLANT	MMO CD 3058
_____ C.P.E. BACH CONCERTO IN A MINOR	MMO CD 3059
_____ STRETCHIN' OUT-'Comping' with a Jazz Rhythm Section	MMO CD 3060
_____ RAVEL: PIANO TRIO	MMO CD 3061
_____ THE JIM ODRICH EXPERIENCE Pop Piano Played Easy	MMO CD 3062
_____ POPULAR PIANO MADE EASY Arranged by Jim Odrich	MMO CD 3063
_____ SCHUMANN: Piano Trio in D Minor, Opus 63	MMO CD 3064
_____ BEETHOVEN: Trio No. 8 & Trio No. 11, "Kakadu" Variations	MMO CD 3065
_____ SCHUBERT: Piano Trio in Bb Major, Opus 99 (2 CD Set)	MMO CD 3066
_____ SCHUBERT: Piano Trio in Eb Major, Opus 100 (2 CD Set)	MMO CD 3067
_____ POPULAR SONGS Arranged by Jim Odrich	MMO CD 3069
_____ BEETHOVEN: QUINTET FOR PIANO in Eb Major, Opus 16	MMO CD 3070
_____ MOZART: QUINTET FOR PIANO in Eb, K.452	MMO CD 3071
_____ MOZART: PIANO CONCERTO #21 IN C MAJOR, K.467	MMO CD 3072
_____ MOZART: PIANO CONCERTO KV 449.	MMO CD 3073

PIANO - FOUR HANDS

_____ RACHMANINOFF Six Scenes	4-5th year	MMO CD 3027
_____ ARENSKY 6 Pieces, STRAVINSKY 3 Easy Dances	2-3rd year	MMO CD 3028
_____ FAURE: The Dolly Suite		MMO CD 3029
_____ DEBUSSY: Four Pieces		MMO CD 3030
_____ SCHUMANN Pictures from the East	4-5th year	MMO CD 3031
_____ BEETHOVEN Three Marches	4-5th year	MMO CD 3032
_____ MOZART COMPLETE MUSIC FOR PIANO FOUR HANDS 2 CD Set		MMO CD 3036
_____ MAYKAPAR First Steps, OP. 29	1-2nd year	MMO CD 3041
_____ TSCHAIKOVSKY: 50 Russian Folk Songs		MMO CD 3042
_____ BIZET: 12 Children's Games		MMO CD 3043
_____ GRETCHANINOFF: ON THE GREEN MEADOW		MMO CD 3044
_____ POZZOLI: SMILES OF CHILDHOOD		MMO CD 3045
_____ DIABELLI: PLEASURES OF YOUTH		MMO CD 3046
_____ SCHUBERT: FANTASIA & GRAND SONATA		MMO CD 3047

VIOLIN

_____ BRUCH CONCERTO NO. 1 IN G MINOR OP.26	MMO CD 3100
_____ MENDELSSOHN CONCERTO IN E MINOR	MMO CD 3101
_____ TSCHAIKOVSKY CONCERTO IN D OP. 35	MMO CD 3102
_____ BACH DOUBLE CONCERTO IN D MINOR	MMO CD 3103
_____ BACH CONCERTO IN A MINOR, CONCERTO IN E	MMO CD 3104
_____ BACH BRANDENBURG CONCERTI NOS. 4 & 5	MMO CD 3105
_____ BACH BRANDENBURG CONCERTO NO. 2, TRIPLE CONCERTO	MMO CD 3106
_____ BACH CONCERTO IN DM, (FROM CONCERTO FOR HARPSICHORD)	MMO CD 3107

MMO Music Group • 50 Executive Boulevard, Elmsford, New York 10523, 1-(800) 669-7464
Website: www. minusone.com • E-mail: mmomus@aol.com

Young At Heart

By Carol Leigh
and Johnny Richards

At the intro, flutes and trombones set the mood. Piano enters with melody in octaves coupled with thirds, block chords, and single-note melody with LH chords. Events here include piano playing a figure with the band, more single-note melody and a change of registers. During the last phrase, I play block chords in the upper register, elaborated melody with fill-ins, and keep changing the textures right to the very end.

MMO CD 3069
Young At Heart - 1

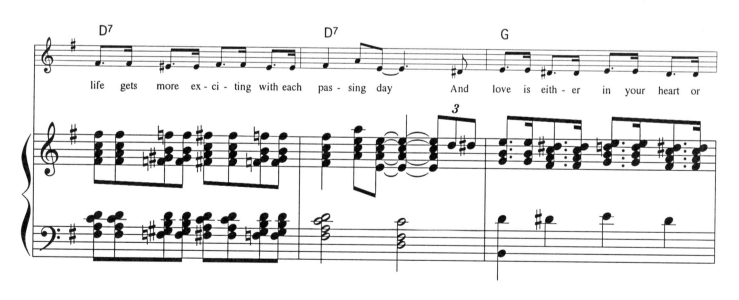

28

It's All Right With Me

30

Words and Music by
Cole Porter

This is a good example of how the pianist can vary both style and texture according to what the background does. Notice that much use is made of single-note melody, melody in octaves one octave apart, and melody in octaves two octaves apart. Chordal voicings, of course, are also used here to good effect. In the last two measures, piano plays the ending brass figure with the band. After listening, try to apply these devices and principles of contrast in your own unique way.   J.O.

MMO CD 3069
It's All Right With Me-1

A♭7
D♭
G9
free, dear, it's all right It's
G♭9
E♭9
A♭11
All Right With Me
D♭
f
mf sfz mf sfz mf sfz ff

MMO Compact Disc Catalog

- BRAHMS CONCERTO IN D OP. 77 — MMO CD 3108
- CHAUSSON POEME, SCHUBERT RONDO — MMO CD 3109
- LALO SYMPHONIE ESPAGNOLE — MMO CD 3110
- MOZART CONCERTO IN D K.218, VIVALDI CON. AM OP.3 NO.6 — MMO CD 3111
- MOZART CONCERTO IN A K.219 — MMO CD 3112
- WIENIAWSKI CON. IN D. SARASATE ZIGEUNERWEISEN — MMO CD 3113
- VIOTTI CONCERTO NO. 22 IN A MINOR — MMO CD 3114
- BEETHOVEN 2 ROMANCES, SONATA NO. 5 IN F "SPRING SONATA" — MMO CD 3115
- SAINT-SAENS INTRODUCTION & RONDO,
- MOZART SERENADE K. 204, ADAGIO K.261 — MMO CD 3116
- BEETHOVEN CONCERTO IN D OP. 61(2 CD SET) — MMO CD 3117
- THE CONCERTMASTER - Orchestral Excerpts — MMO CD 3118
- AIR ON A G STRING Favorite Encores with Orchestra Easy Medium — MMO CD 3119
- CONCERT PIECES FOR THE SERIOUS VIOLINIST Easy Medium — MMO CD 3120
- 18TH CENTURY VIOLIN PIECES — MMO CD 3121
- ORCHESTRAL FAVORITES - Volume 1 - Easy Level — MMO CD 3122
- ORCHESTRAL FAVORITES - Volume 2 - Medium Level — MMO CD 3123
- ORCHESTRAL FAVORITES - Volume 3 - Med to Difficult Level — MMO CD 3124
- THE THREE B'S BACH/BEETHOVEN/BRAHMS — MMO CD 3125
- VIVALDI: VIOLIN CONCERTOS — MMO CD 3126
- VIVALDI-THE FOUR SEASONS (2 CD Set) — MMO CD 3127
- VIVALDI Concerto in Eb, Op. 8, No. 5. ALBINONI Concerto in A — MMO CD 3128
- VIVALDI Concerto in E, Op. 3, No. 12. Concerto in C Op. 8, No.6 "Il Piacere" — MMO CD 3129
- SCHUBERT Three Sonatinas — MMO CD 3130
- HAYDN String Quartet Op. 76 No. 1 — MMO CD 3131
- HAYDN String Quartet Op. 76 No. 2 — MMO CD 3132
- HAYDN String Quartet Op. 76 No. 3 "Emperor" — MMO CD 3133
- HAYDN String Quartet Op. 76 No. 4 "Sunrise" — MMO CD 3134
- HAYDN String Quartet Op. 76 No. 5 — MMO CD 3135
- HAYDN String Quartet Op. 76 No. 6 — MMO CD 3136
- BEAUTIFUL MUSIC FOR TWO VIOLINS 1st position, vol. 1 — MMO CD 3137*
- BEAUTIFUL MUSIC FOR TWO VIOLINS 2nd position, vol. 2 — MMO CD 3138*
- BEAUTIFUL MUSIC FOR TWO VIOLINS 3rd position, vol. 3 — MMO CD 3139*
- BEAUTIFUL MUSIC FOR TWO VIOLINS 1st, 2nd, 3rd position, vol. 4 — MMO CD 3140*

*Lovely folk tunes and selections from the classics, chosen for their melodic beauty and technical value. They have been skillfully transcribed and edited by Samuel Applebaum, one of America's foremost teachers.

- HEART OF THE VIOLIN CONCERTO — MMO CD 3141
- TEACHER'S PARTNER Basic Violin Studies 1st year — MMO CD 3142
- DVORAK STRING TRIO "Terzetto", OP. 74 2 violins/viola — MMO CD 3143
- SIBELIUS: Concerto in D minor, Op. 47 — MMO CD 3144
- THEMES FROM THE MAJOR VIOLIN CONCERTI — MMO CD 3145
- STRAVINSKY: L'HISTOIRE DU SOLDAT — MMO CD 3146
- RAVEL: PIANO TRIO MINUS VIOLIN — MMO CD 3147
- GREAT VIOLIN MOMENTS — MMO CD 3148
- RAGTIME STRING QUARTETS The Zinn String Quartet — MMO CD 3151
- SCHUMANN: Piano Trio in D minor, Opus 63 — MMO CD 3152
- BEETHOVEN: Trio No. 8 & Trio No. 11, "Kakadu" Variations — MMO CD 3153
- SCHUBERT: Piano Trio in Bb Major, Opus 99 Minus Violin (2 CD Set) — MMO CD 3154
- SCHUBERT: Piano Trio in Eb Major, Opus 100 Minus Violin (2 CD Set) — MMO CD 3155
- BEETHOVEN: STRING QUARTET in A minor, Opus 132 (2 CD Set) — MMO CD 3156
- DVORAK QUINTET in A major, Opus 81 Minus Violin — MMO CD 3157
- BEETHOVEN: STRING QTS No. 1 in F major & No. 4 in C minor, Opus 18 — MMO CD 3158
- HAYDN Three Trios with Piano & Cello — MMO CD 3159
- MOZART: CONCERTO NO. 3 FOR VIOLIN AND ORCHESTRA. — MMO CD 3160
- MISCHA ELMAN FAVORITE ENCORES. — MMO CD 3162
- MISCHA ELMAN CONCERT FAVORITES. — MMO CD 3163
- JASCHA HEIFETZ FAVORITE ENCORES. — MMO CD 3164
- FRITZ KREISLER FAVORITE ENCORES — MMO CD 3165

GUITAR

- BOCCHERINI Quintet No. 4 in D "Fandango" — MMO CD 3601
- GIULIANI Quintet in A Op. 65 — MMO CD 3602
- CLASSICAL GUITAR DUETS — MMO CD 3603
- RENAISSANCE & BAROQUE GUITAR DUETS — MMO CD 3604
- CLASSICAL & ROMANTIC GUITAR DUETS — MMO CD 3605
- GUITAR AND FLUTE DUETS Volume 1 — MMO CD 3606
- GUITAR AND FLUTE DUETS Volume 2 — MMO CD 3607
- BLUEGRASS GUITAR — MMO CD 3608
- GEORGE BARNES GUITAR METHOD Lessons from a Master — MMO CD 3609
- HOW TO PLAY FOLK GUITAR 2 CD Set — MMO CD 3610
- FAVORITE FOLKS SONGS FOR GUITAR — MMO CD 3611
- FOR GUITARS ONLY! Jimmy Raney Small Band Arrangements — MMO CD 3612
- TEN DUETS FOR TWO GUITARS Geo. Barnes/Carl Kress — MMO CD 3613
- PLAY THE BLUES GUITAR A Dick Weissman Method — MMO CD 3614
- ORCHESTRAL GEMS FOR CLASSICAL GUITAR — MMO CD 3615

FLUTE

- MOZART Concerto No. 2 in D, QUANTZ Concerto in G — MMO CD 3300
- MOZART Concerto in G K.313 — MMO CD 3301
- BACH Suite No. 2 in B Minor — MMO CD 3302
- BOCCHERINI Concerto in D, VIVALDI Concerto in G Minor "La Notte",
- MOZART Andante for Strings — MMO CD 3303
- HAYDN Divertimento, VIVALDI Concerto in D Op. 10 No. 3 "Bullfinch",
- FREDERICK THE GREAT Concerto in C — MMO CD 3304
- VIVALDI Conc. in F; TELEMANN Conc. in D; LECLAIR Conc. in C — MMO CD 3305
- BACH Brandenburg No. 2 in F, HAYDN Concerto in D — MMO CD 3306
- BACH Triple Concerto, VIVALDI Concerto in D Minor — MMO CD 3307
- MOZART Quartet in F, STAMITZ Quartet in F — MMO CD 3308
- HAYDN 4 London Trios for 2 Flutes & Cello — MMO CD 3309
- BACH Brandenburg Concerti Nos. 4 & 5 — MMO CD 3310
- MOZART 3 Flute Quartets in D, A and C — MMO CD 3311
- TELEMANN Suite in A Minor, GLUCK Scene from 'Orpheus',
- PERGOLESI Concerto in G (2 CD Set) — MMO CD 3312
- FLUTE SONG: Easy Familiar Classics — MMO CD 3313
- VIVALDI Concerti In D, G, and F — MMO CD 3314
- VIVALDI Concerti in A Minor, G, and D — MMO CD 3315
- EASY FLUTE SOLOS Beginning Students Volume 1 — MMO CD 3316
- EASY FLUTE SOLOS Beginning Students Volume 2 — MMO CD 3317
- EASY JAZZ DUETS Student Level — MMO CD 3318
- FLUTE & GUITAR DUETS Volume 1 — MMO CD 3319
- FLUTE & GUITAR DUETS Volume 2 — MMO CD 3320
- BEGINNING CONTEST SOLOS Murray Panitz — MMO CD 3321
- BEGINNING CONTEST SOLOS Donald Peck — MMO CD 3322
- INTERMEDIATE CONTEST SOLOS Julius Baker — MMO CD 3323
- INTERMEDIATE CONTEST SOLOS Donald Peck — MMO CD 3324
- ADVANCED CONTEST SOLOS Murray Panitz — MMO CD 3325
- ADVANCED CONTEST SOLOS Julius Baker — MMO CD 3326
- INTERMEDIATE CONTEST SOLOS Donald Peck — MMO CD 3327
- ADVANCED CONTEST SOLOS Murray Panitz — MMO CD 3328
- ADVANCED CONTEST SOLOS Julius Baker — MMO CD 3329
- BEGINNING CONTEST SOLOS Doriot Anthony Dwyer — MMO CD 3330
- INTERMEDIATE CONTEST SOLOS Doriot Anthony Dwyer — MMO CD 3331
- ADVANCED CONTEST SOLOS Doriot Anthony Dwyer — MMO CD 3332
- FIRST CHAIR SOLOS with Orchestral Accompaniment — MMO CD 3333
- TEACHER'S PARTNER Basic Flute Studies 1st year — MMO CD 3334
- THE JOY OF WOODWIND MUSIC — MMO CD 3335
- JEWELS FOR WOODWIND QUINTET — MMO CD 3336
- TELEMANN TRIO IN F/Bb MAJOR/HANDEL SON.#3 IN C MAJOR — MMO CD 3340
- MARCELLO/TELEMANN/HANDEL SONATAS IN F MAJOR — MMO CD 3341
- BOLLING: SUITE FOR FLUTE/JAZZ PIANO TRIO — MMO CD 3342
- HANDEL / TELEMANN SIX SONATAS 2 CD Set — MMO CD 3343
- BACH SONATA NO. 1 in B MINOR/KUHLAU E MINOR DUET (2 CD set) — MMO CD 3344
- KUHLAU TRIO in Eb MAJOR/BACH Eb AND A MAJOR SONATA (2 CD set) — MMO CD 3345
- PEPUSCH SONATA IN C / TELEMANN SONATA IN Cm — MMO CD 3346
- QUANTZ TRIO SONATA IN Cm / BACH GIGUE / ABEL SON. 2 IN F — MMO CD 3347
- TELEMANN CONCERTO NO. 1 IN D / CORRETTE SONATA IN E MINOR — MMO CD 3348
- TELEMANN TRIO IN F / Bb MAJOR / HANDEL SON. #3 IN C MAJOR — MMO CD 3349
- MARCELLO / TELEMANN / HANDEL SONATAS IN F MAJOR — MMO CD 3350
- CONCERT BAND FAVORITES WITH ORCHESTRA — MMO CD 3351
- BAND-AIDS CONCERT BAND FAVORITES WITH ORCHESTRA — MMO CD 3352
- UNSUNG HERO George Roberts — MMO CD 3353
- WORLD FAVORITES Student Editions, 41 Easy Selections (1st-2nd year) — MMO CD 3354
- CLASSIC THEMES Student Editions, 27 Easy Songs (2nd-3rd year) — MMO CD 3355

RECORDER

- PLAYING THE RECORDER Folk Songs of Many Nations — MMO CD 3337
- LET'S PLAY THE RECORDER Beginning Children's Method — MMO CD 3338
- YOU CAN PLAY THE RECORDER Beginning Adult Method — MMO CD 3339

FRENCH HORN

- MOZART: Concerti No. 2 & No. 3 in Eb. K. 417 & 447 — MMO CD 3501
- BAROQUE BRASS AND BEYOND — MMO CD 3502
- MUSIC FOR BRASS ENSEMBLE — MMO CD 3503
- MOZART: Sonatas for Two Horns — MMO CD 3504
- BEETHOVEN: QUINTET FOR FRENCH HORN in Eb Major, Opus 16 — MMO CD 3505
- MOZART: QUINTET FOR FRENCH HORN in Eb, K.452 — MMO CD 3506
- BEGINNING CONTEST SOLOS Mason Jones — MMO CD 3511
- BEGINNING CONTEST SOLOS Myron Bloom — MMO CD 3512
- INTERMEDIATE CONTEST SOLOS Dale Clevenger — MMO CD 3513
- INTERMEDIATE CONTEST SOLOS Mason Jones — MMO CD 3514
- ADVANCED CONTEST SOLOS Myron Bloom — MMO CD 3515
- ADVANCED CONTEST SOLOS Dale Clevenger — MMO CD 3516
- INTERMEDIATE CONTEST SOLOS Mason Jones — MMO CD 3517
- ADVANCED CONTEST SOLOS Myron Bloom — MMO CD 3518
- INTERMEDIATE CONTEST SOLOS Dale Clevenger — MMO CD 3519
- FRENCH HORN WOODWIND MUSIC — MMO CD 3520
- MASTERPIECES FOR WOODWIND QUINTET — MMO CD 3521
- FRENCH HORN UP FRONT BRASS QUINTETS — MMO CD 3522
- HORN OF PLENTY BRASS QUINTETS — MMO CD 3523
- BAND-AIDS CONCERT BAND FAVORITES WITH ORCHESTRA — MMO CD 3524

MMO Music Group • 50 Executive Boulevard, Elmsford, New York 10523, 1-(800) 669-7464
Website: www. minusone.com • E-mail: mmomus@aol.com

This Is All I Ask

Words and Music by
Gordon Jenkins

The piano picks up the mood of the orchestra's intro, and follows the lead of the ad-lib portion of the light string background with varied melodic textures to sustain the listener's interest: melody in octaves and single notes, first with arpeggiated LH bass, then with held LH chords. When the rhythm section enters to establish tempo, I am careful to use thinner textures to allow some of the attractive background figures to sound through. J.O.

42

MMO Compact Disc Catalog

TRUMPET

____ THREE CONCERTI: HAYDN, TELEMANN, FASCH ....MMO CD 3801
____ TRUMPET SOLOS Student Level Volume 1 ....MMO CD 3802
____ TRUMPET SOLOS Student Level Volume 2 ....MMO CD 3803
____ EASY JAZZ DUETS Student Level ....MMO CD 3804
____ MUSIC FOR BRASS ENSEMBLE Brass Quintets............................MMO CD 3805
____ FIRST CHAIR TRUMPET SOLOS with Orchestral Accompaniment ....MMO CD 3806
____ THE ART OF THE SOLO TRUMPET with Orchestral Accompaniment ....MMO CD 3807
____ BAROQUE BRASS AND BEYOND Brass Quintets ....MMO CD 3808
____ THE COMPLETE ARBAN DUETS all of the classic studies...............MMO CD 3809
____ SOUSA MARCHES PLUS BEETHOVEN, BERLIOZ, STRAUSS ....MMO CD 3810
____ BEGINNING CONTEST SOLOS Gerard Schwarz ....MMO CD 3811
____ BEGINNING CONTEST SOLOS Armando Ghitalla ....MMO CD 3812
____ INTERMEDIATE CONTEST SOLOS Robert Nagel, Soloist ....MMO CD 3813
____ INTERMEDIATE CONTEST SOLOS Gerard Schwarz ....MMO CD 3814
____ ADVANCED CONTEST SOLOS Robert Nagel, Soloist ....MMO CD 3815
____ CONTEST SOLOS Armando Ghitalla ....MMO CD 3816
____ INTERMEDIATE CONTEST SOLOS Gerard Schwarz ....MMO CD 3817
____ ADVANCED CONTEST SOLOS Robert Nagel, Soloist ....MMO CD 3818
____ ADVANCED CONTEST SOLOS Armando Ghitalla ....MMO CD 3819
____ BEGINNING CONTEST SOLOS Raymond Crisara ....MMO CD 3820
____ BEGINNING CONTEST SOLOS Raymond Crisara ....MMO CD 3821
____ INTERMEDIATE CONTEST SOLOS Raymond Crisara ....MMO CD 3822
____ TEACHER'S PARTNER Basic Trumpet Studies 1st year ....MMO CD 3823
____ TWENTY DIXIELAND CLASSICS ....MMO CD 3824
____ TWENTY RHYTHM BACKGROUNDS TO STANDARDS ....MMO CD 3825
____ FROM DIXIE TO SWING ....MMO CD 3826
____ TRUMPET PIECES BRASS QUINTETS ....MMO CD 3827
____ MODERN BRASS QUINTETS ....MMO CD 3828
____ WHEN JAZZ WAS YOUNG The Bob Wilber All Stars ....MMO CD 3829
____ CLASSIC TRUMPET SELECTIONS WITH PIANO ....MMO CD 3830
____ CONCERT BAND FAVORITES WITH ORCHESTRA ....MMO CD 3831
____ BAND-AIDS CONCERT BAND FAVORITES WITH ORCHESTRA ....MMO CD 3832
____ BRASS TRAX The Trumpet Artistry Of David O'Neill ....MMO CD 3833
____ TRUMPET TRIUMPHANT The Further Adventures Of David O'Neill ....MMO CD 3834
____ WORLD FAVORITES Student Editions, 41 Easy Selections (1st-2nd year) ......MMO CD 3836
____ CLASSIC THEMES Student Editions, 27 Easy Songs (2nd-3rd year) ....MMO CD 3837
____ STRAVINSKY: L'HISTOIRE DU SOLDAT ....MMO CD 3835
____ 12 CLASSIC JAZZ STANDARDS Bb/Eb/Bass Clef.......................MMO CD 7010
____ 12 MORE CLASSIC JAZZ STANDARDS Bb/Eb/Bass Clef................MMO CD 7011

TROMBONE

____ TROMBONE SOLOS Student Level Volume 1 ....MMO CD 3901
____ TROMBONE SOLOS Student Level Volume 2 ....MMO CD 3902
____ EASY JAZZ DUETS Student Level ....MMO CD 3903
____ BAROQUE BRASS & BEYOND Brass Quintets............................MMO CD 3904
____ MUSIC FOR BRASS ENSEMBLE Brass Quintets ....MMO CD 3905
____ UNSUNG HERO George Roberts ....MMO CD 3906
____ BIG BAND BALLADS George Roberts ....MMO CD 3907
____ STRAVINSKY: L'HISTOIRE DU SOLDAT ....MMO CD 3908
____ CLASSICAL TROMBONE SOLOS ....MMO CD 3909
____ JAZZ STANDARDS WITH STRINGS (2 CD Set) ....MMO CD 3910
____ BEGINNING CONTEST SOLOS Per Brevig ....MMO CD 3911
____ BEGINNING CONTEST SOLOS Jay Friedman............................MMO CD 3912
____ INTERMEDIATE CONTEST SOLOS Keith Brown, Professor, Indiana U. ......MMO CD 3913
____ INTERMEDIATE CONTEST SOLOS Jay Friedman ....MMO CD 3914
____ ADVANCED CONTEST SOLOS Keith Brown, Professor, Indiana University ..MMO CD 3915
____ ADVANCED CONTEST SOLOS Per Brevig ....MMO CD 3916
____ ADVANCED CONTEST SOLOS Keith Brown, Professor, Indiana University ..MMO CD 3917
____ ADVANCED CONTEST SOLOS Jay Friedman ....MMO CD 3918
____ ADVANCED CONTEST SOLOS Per Brevig ....MMO CD 3919
____ TEACHER'S PARTNER Basic Trombone Studies 1st year ....MMO CD 3920
____ TWENTY DIXIELAND CLASSICS ....MMO CD 3924
____ TWENTY RHYTHM BACKGROUNDS TO STANDARDS ....MMO CD 3925
____ FROM DIXIE TO SWING ....MMO CD 3926
____ STICKS & BONES BRASS QUINTETS......................................MMO CD 3927
____ FOR TROMBONES ONLY MORE BRASS QUINTETS ....MMO CD 3928
____ POPULAR CONCERT FAVORITES The Stuttgart Festival Band ......MMO CD 3929
____ BAND-AIDS CONCERT BAND FAVORITES WITH ORCHESTRA ....MMO CD 3930
____ WORLD FAVORITES Student Editions, 41 Easy Selections (1st-2nd year) ......MMO CD 3931
____ CLASSIC THEMES Student Editions, 27 Easy Songs (2nd-3rd year) ....MMO CD 3932
____ 12 CLASSIC JAZZ STANDARDS Bb/Eb/Bass Clef.......................MMO CD 7010
____ 12 MORE CLASSIC JAZZ STANDARDS Bb/Eb/Bass Clef................MMO CD 7011

TENOR SAXOPHONE

____ TENOR SAXOPHONE SOLOS Student Edition Volume 1 ....MMO CD 4201
____ TENOR SAXOPHONE SOLOS Student Edition Volume 2 ....MMO CD 4202
____ EASY JAZZ DUETS FOR TENOR SAXOPHONE ....MMO CD 4203
____ FOR SAXES ONLY Arranged by Bob Wilber..............................MMO CD 4204
____ BLUES FUSION FOR SAXOPHONE ....MMO CD 4205

____ JOBIM BRAZILIAN BOSSA NOVAS with STRINGS ....MMO CD 4206
____ TWENTY DIXIE CLASSICS..MMO CD 4207
____ TWENTY RHYTHM BACKGROUNDS TO STANDARDS ....MMO CD 4208
____ PLAY LEAD IN A SAX SECTION ....MMO CD 4209
____ DAYS OF WINE & ROSES Sax Section Minus You ....MMO CD 4210
____ FRENCH & AMERICAN SAXOPHONE QUARTETS ....MMO CD 4211
____ CONCERT BAND FAVORITES WITH ORCHESTRA ....MMO CD 4212
____ BAND AIDS CONCERT BAND FAVORITES...............................MMO CD 4213
____ JAZZ JAM FOR TENOR (2 CD Set) ....MMO CD 4214
____ 12 CLASSIC JAZZ STANDARDS Bb/Eb/Bass Clef.......................MMO CD 7010
____ 12 MORE CLASSIC JAZZ STANDARDS Bb/Eb/Bass Clef................MMO CD 7011

CELLO

____ DVORAK Concerto in B Minor Op. 104 (2 CD Set) ....MMO CD 3701
____ C.P.E. BACH Concerto in A Minor ....MMO CD 3702
____ BOCCHERINI Concerto in Bb, BRUCH Kol Nidrei ....MMO CD 3703
____ TEN PIECES FOR CELLO ....MMO CD 3704
____ SCHUMANN Concerto in Am & Other Selections ....MMO CD 3705
____ CLAUDE BOLLING Suite For Cello & Jazz Piano Trio ....MMO CD 3706
____ RAVEL: PIANO TRIO MINUS CELLO ....MMO CD 3707
____ RAGTIME STRING QUARTETS ....MMO CD 3708
____ SCHUMANN: Piano Trio in D Minor, Opus 63 ....MMO CD 3709
____ BEETHOVEN: Piano Trio For Cello ....MMO CD 3710
____ SCHUBERT: Piano Trio in Bb Major, Opus 99 Minus Cello (2 CD Set) ....MMO CD 3711
____ SCHUBERT: Piano Trio in Eb Major, Opus 100 Minus Cello (2 CD Set) ....MMO CD 3712
____ BEETHOVEN: STRING QUARTET in A minor, Opus 132 (2 CD Set) ....MMO CD 3713
____ DVORAK QUINTET in A Major, Opus 81 Minus Cello....................MMO CD 3714
____ BEETHOVEN: SONATA IN A MAJOR, OP. 69 Minus Cello ....MMO CD 3715
____ WINER: Concerto/SCHUBERT: Ave Maria/SAINT-SAENS: Allegro Appass. ..MMO CD 3716

OBOE

____ ALBINONI Concerti in Bb, Op. 7 No. 3, No. 6, D. Op. 9 No. 2 in Dm ....MMO CD 3400
____ TELEMANN Conc. in Fm; HANDEL Conc. in Bb; VIVALDI Conc.in Dm ....MMO CD 3401
____ MOZART Quartet in F K.370, STAMITZ Quartet in F Op. 8 No. 3 ....MMO CD 3402
____ BACH Brandenburg Concerto No. 2, Telemann Con. in Am ....MMO CD 3403
____ CLASSIC SOLOS FOR OBOE Delia Montenegro, Soloist ....MMO CD 3404
____ MASTERPIECES FOR WOODWIND QUINTET ....MMO CD 3405
____ THE JOY OF WOODWIND QUINTETS.......................................MMO CD 3406
____ PEPUSCH SONATAS IN C/TELEMANN SONATA IN Cm ....MMO CD 3407
____ QUANTZ TRIO SONATA IN Cm/BACH GIGUE/ABEL SONATAS IN F ....MMO CD 3408
____ BEETHOVEN: QUINTET FOR OBOE in Eb, Opus 16 ....MMO CD 3409

ALTO SAXOPHONE

____ ALTO SAXOPHONE SOLOS Student Edition Volume 1 ....MMO CD 4101
____ ALTO SAXOPHONE SOLOS Student Edition Volume 2. ....MMO CD 4102
____ EASY JAZZ DUETS FOR ALTO SAXOPHONE ....MMO CD 4103
____ FOR SAXES ONLY Arranged Bob Wilber ....MMO CD 4104
____ JOBIM BRAZILIAN BOSSA NOVAS with STRINGS ....MMO CD 4106
____ UNSUNG HEROES FOR ALTO SAXOPHONE..............................MMO CD 4107
____ BEGINNING CONTEST SOLOS Paul Brodie, Canadian Soloist .....MMO CD 4111
____ BEGINNING CONTEST SOLOS Vincent Abato ....MMO CD 4112
____ INTERMEDIATE CONTEST SOLOS Paul Brodie, Canadian Soloist ....MMO CD 4113
____ INTERMEDIATE CONTEST SOLOS Vincent Abato ....MMO CD 4114
____ ADVANCED CONTEST SOLOS Paul Brodie, Canadian Soloist.......MMO CD 4115
____ ADVANCED CONTEST SOLOS Vincent Abato ....MMO CD 4116
____ ADVANCED CONTEST SOLOS Paul Brodie, Canadian Soloist ......MMO CD 4117
____ Basic Studies for Alto Sax TEACHER'S PARTNER 1st year level ....MMO CD 4119
____ ADVANCED CONTEST SOLOS Vincent Abato ....MMO CD 4118
____ PLAY LEAD IN A SAX SECTION ....MMO CD 4120
____ DAYS OF WINE & ROSES/SENSUAL SAX ....MMO CD 4121
____ TWENTY DIXIELAND CLASSICS ....MMO CD 4124
____ TWENTY RHYTHM BACKGROUNDS TO STANDARDS ....MMO CD 4125
____ CONCERT BAND FAVORITES WITH ORCHESTRA ....MMO CD 4126
____ BAND AIDS CONCERT BAND FAVORITES...............................MMO CD 4127
____ MUSIC FOR SAXOPHONE QUARTET ....MMO CD 4128
____ WORLD FAVORITES Student Editions, 41 Easy Selections (1st-2nd year) ......MMO CD 4129
____ CLASSIC THEMES Student Editions, 27 Easy Songs (2nd-3rd year) ....MMO CD 4130
____ 12 CLASSIC JAZZ STANDARDS Bb/Eb/Bass Clef.......................MMO CD 7010
____ 12 MORE CLASSIC JAZZ STANDARDS Bb/Eb/Bass Clef................MMO CD 7011

SOPRANO SAXOPHONE

____ FRENCH & AMERICAN SAXOPHONE QUARTETS ....MMO CD 4801
____ 12 CLASSIC JAZZ STANDARDS Bb/Eb/Bass Clef.......................MMO CD 7010
____ 12 MORE CLASSIC JAZZ STANDARDS Bb/Eb/Bass Clef................MMO CD 7011

MMO Music Group • 50 Executive Boulevard, Elmsford, New York 10523, 1-(800) 669-7464
Website: www. minusone.com • E-mail: mmomus@aol.com

The Best Is Yet To Come

Music by Cy Coleman
Lyric by Carolyn Leigh

This is a very good example of how the pianist varies both style and texture according to what the background does. After listening, try to achieve this contrast in your own way.   J.O.

MMO CD 3069
The Best Is Yet To Come - 1

45

MMO Compact Disc Catalog

BARITONE SAXOPHONE

_____ MUSIC FOR SAXOPHONE QUARTET ....MMO CD 4901
_____ 12 CLASSIC JAZZ STANDARDS Bb/Eb/Bass Clef.................MMO CD 7010
_____ 12 MORE CLASSIC JAZZ STANDARDS Bb/Eb/Bass Clef................MMO CD 7011

VOCAL

_____ SCHUBERT GERMAN LIEDER - High Voice, Volume 1 ....MMO CD 4001
_____ SCHUBERT GERMAN LIEDER - Low Voice, Volume 1 ....MMO CD 4002
_____ SCHUBERT GERMAN LIEDER - High Voice, Volume 2 ....MMO CD 4003
_____ SCHUBERT GERMAN LIEDER - Low Voice, Volume 2 ....MMO CD 4004
_____ BRAHMS GERMAN LIEDER - High Voice ....MMO CD 4005
_____ BRAHMS GERMAN LIEDER - Low Voice ....MMO CD 4006
_____ EVERYBODY'S FAVORITE SONGS - High Voice, Volume 1 ....MMO CD 4007
_____ EVERYBODY'S FAVORITE SONGS - Low Voice, Volume 1 ....MMO CD 4008
_____ EVERYBODY'S FAVORITE SONGS - High Voice, Volume 2 ....MMO CD 4009
_____ EVERYBODY'S FAVORITE SONGS - Low Voice, Volume 2 ....MMO CD 4010
_____ 17th/18th CENT. ITALIAN SONGS - High Voice, Volume 1 ....MMO CD 4011
_____ 17th/18th CENT. ITALIAN SONGS - Low Voice, Volume 1 ....MMO CD 4012
_____ 17th/18th CENT. ITALIAN SONGS - High Voice, Volume 2 ....MMO CD 4013
_____ 17th/18th CENT. ITALIAN SONGS - Low Voice, Volume 2 ....MMO CD 4014
_____ FAMOUS SOPRANO ARIAS ....MMO CD 4015
_____ FAMOUS MEZZO-SOPRANO ARIAS ....MMO CD 4016
_____ FAMOUS TENOR ARIAS ....MMO CD 4017
_____ FAMOUS BARITONE ARIAS ....MMO CD 4018
_____ FAMOUS BASS ARIAS ....MMO CD 4019
_____ WOLF GERMAN LIEDER FOR HIGH VOICE ....MMO CD 4020
_____ WOLF GERMAN LIEDER FOR LOW VOICE ....MMO CD 4021
_____ STRAUSS GERMAN LIEDER FOR HIGH VOICE...............................MMO CD 4022
_____ STRAUSS GERMAN LIEDER FOR LOW VOICE ....MMO CD 4023
_____ SCHUMANN GERMAN LIEDER FOR HIGH VOICE ....MMO CD 4024
_____ SCHUMANN GERMAN LIEDER FOR LOW VOICE ....MMO CD 4025
_____ MOZART ARIAS FOR SOPRANO ....MMO CD 4026
_____ VERDI ARIAS FOR SOPRANO..MMO CD 4027
_____ ITALIAN ARIAS FOR SOPRANO ....MMO CD 4028
_____ FRENCH ARIAS FOR SOPRANO ....MMO CD 4029
_____ ORATORIO ARIAS FOR SOPRANO ....MMO CD 4030
_____ ORATORIO ARIAS FOR ALTO ....MMO CD 4031
_____ ORATORIO ARIAS FOR TENOR ....MMO CD 4032
_____ ORATORIO ARIAS FOR BASS ....MMO CD 4033
_____ BEGINNING SOPRANO SOLOS Kate Hurney ....MMO CD 4041
_____ INTERMEDIATE SOPRANO SOLOS Kate Hurney ....MMO CD 4042
_____ BEGINNING MEZZO SOPRANO SOLOS Fay Kittelson ....MMO CD 4043
_____ INTERMEDIATE MEZZO SOPRANO SOLOS Fay Kittelson...................MMO CD 4044
_____ ADVANCED MEZZO SOPRANO SOLOS Fay Kittelson ....MMO CD 4045
_____ BEGINNING CONTRALTO SOLOS Carline Ray ....MMO CD 4046
_____ BEGINNING TENOR SOLOS George Shirley ....MMO CD 4047
_____ INTERMEDIATE TENOR SOLOS George Shirley ....MMO CD 4048
_____ ADVANCED TENOR SOLOS George Shirley ....MMO CD 4049
_____ TWELVE CLASSIC VOCAL STANDARDS, VOL.1 ....MMO CD 4050
_____ TWELVE CLASSIC VOCAL STANDARDS, VOL.2 ....MMO CD 4051
_____ SOPRANO ARIAS WITH ORCHESTRA The Viidin Philharmonic Orch..........MMO CD 4052
_____ PUCCINI ARIAS FOR SOPRANO WITH ORCHESTRA ....MMO CD 4053
_____ SOPRANO ARIAS WITH ORCHESTRA The Sofia Festival Orch. ....MMO CD 4054
_____ VERDI ARIAS FOR MEZZO-SOPRANO WITH ORCHESTRA ....MMO CD 4055
_____ BASS-BARITONE ARIAS WITH ORCHESTRA. ....MMO CD 4056
_____ TENOR OPERA ARIAS WITH ORCHESTRA ....MMO CD 4057
_____ SOPRANO OPERA ARIAS WITH ORCHESTRA ....MMO CD 4058

DOUBLE BASS

_____ BEGINNING TO INTERMEDIATE CONTEST SOLOS David Walter ....MMO CD 4301
_____ INTERMEDIATE TO ADVANCED CONTEST SOLOS David Walter ....MMO CD 4302
_____ FOR BASSISTS ONLY Ken Smith, Soloist ....MMO CD 4303
_____ THE BEAT GOES ON Jazz - Funk, Latin, Pop-Rock....................MMO CD 4304
_____ FROM DIXIE TO SWING ....MMO CD 4305
_____ STRAVINSKY: L'HISTOIRE DU SOLDAT ....MMO CD 4306

DRUMS

_____ MODERN JAZZ DRUMMING 2 CD Set ....MMO CD 5001
_____ FOR DRUMMERS ONLY ....MMO CD 5002
_____ WIPE OUT ....MMO CD 5003
_____ SIT-IN WITH JIM CHAPIN ....MMO CD 5004
_____ DRUM STAR Trios/Quartets/Quintets Minus You......................MMO CD 5005
_____ DRUMPADSTICKSKIN Jazz play-alongs with small groups ....MMO CD 5006
_____ JUMP & SWING DRUMS ....MMO CD 5007
_____ CLASSICAL PERCUSSION 2 CD Set ....MMO CD 5009
_____ EIGHT MEN IN SEARCH OF A DRUMMER ....MMO CD 5010

_____ FROM DIXIE TO SWING ....MMO CD 5011
_____ FABULOUS SOUNDS OF ROCK DRUMS ....MMO CD 5012
_____ OPEN SESSION WITH THE GREG BURROWS QUINTET (2 CD Set) ....MMO CD 5013
_____ STRAVINSKY: L'HISTOIRE DU SOLDAT ....MMO CD 5014

VIOLA

_____ VIOLA SOLOS with piano accompaniment ....MMO CD 4501
_____ DVORAK STRING TRIO "Terzetto", OP. 74 2 Vins/Viola ....MMO CD 4502
_____ BEETHOVEN: STRING QUARTET in A minor, Opus 132 (2 CD Set) ....MMO CD 4503
_____ DVORAK QUINTET in A major, Opus 81 Minus Viola ....MMO CD 4504
_____ VIOLA CONCERTI WITH ORCHESTRA J.C. Bach/j\Hofmaister ....MMO CD 4505

VIBES

_____ FOR VIBISTS ONLY ....MMO CD 5101
_____ GOOD VIB-RATIONS ....MMO CD 5102

BASSOON

_____ SOLOS FOR THE BASSOON Janet Grice, Soloist ....MMO CD 4601
_____ MASTERPIECES FOR WOODWIND MUSIC ....MMO CD 4602
_____ THE JOY OF WOODWIND QUINTETS......................................MMO CD 4603
_____ STRAVINSKY: L'HISTOIRE DU SOLDAT ....MMO CD 4604
_____ BEETHOVEN: QUINTET FOR BASSOON in Eb, Opus 16.....................MMO CD 4605
_____ MOZART: QUINTET FOR BASSOON in Eb, K.452 ....MMO CD 4606

BANJO

_____ BLUEGRASS BANJO Classic & Favorite Banjo Pieces ....MMO CD 4401
_____ PLAY THE FIVE STRING BANJO Vol. 1 Dick Weissman Method ....MMO CD 4402
_____ PLAY THE FIVE STRING BANJO Vol. 2 Dick Weissman Method ....MMO CD 4403

TUBA or BASS TROMBONE

_____ HE'S NOT HEAVY, HE'S MY TUBA ....MMO CD 4701
_____ SWEETS FOR BRASS ....MMO CD 4702
_____ MUSIC FOR BRASS ENSEMBLE ....MMO CD 4703

INSTRUCTIONAL METHODS

_____ RUTGERS UNIVERSITY MUSIC DICTATION/EAR TRAINING (7 CD Set) ....MMO CD 7001
_____ EVOLUTION OF THE BLUES ....MMO CD 7004
_____ THE ART OF IMPROVISATION, VOL. 1 ....MMO CD 7005
_____ THE ART OF IMPROVISATION, VOL. 2 ....MMO CD 7006
_____ THE BLUES MINUS YOU Ed Xiques, Soloist ....MMO CD 7007
_____ TAKE A CHORUS minus Bb/Eb Instruments.............................MMO CD 7008
_____ UNDERSTANDING JAZZ ....MMO CD 7009
_____ 12 CLASSIC JAZZ STANDARDS Bb/Eb/Bass Clef.........................MMO CD 7010
_____ 12 MORE CLASSIC JAZZ STANDARDS Bb/Eb/Bass Clef....................MMO CD 7011

MMO Music Group • 50 Executive Boulevard, Elmsford, New York 10523, 1-(800) 669-7464
Website: www. minusone.com • E-mail: mmomus@aol.com

All The Way

Words and Music by
Sammy Cahn and
Jimmy Van Heusen

After a gentle orchestral intro, the piano continues the delicate mood with single-note RH melody, first with arpeggiated LH and then with supporting LH chords. Notice how the piano constantly responds to the changes in background style. At one point, I play a long fill-in figure as the background slows down before going back to tempo. When the style later becomes symphonic, I respond with symphonic pianistic voicings and figures. At the very end, the piano plays the final figure with the orchestra. J.O.

MMO CD 3069
All the Way - 1

52

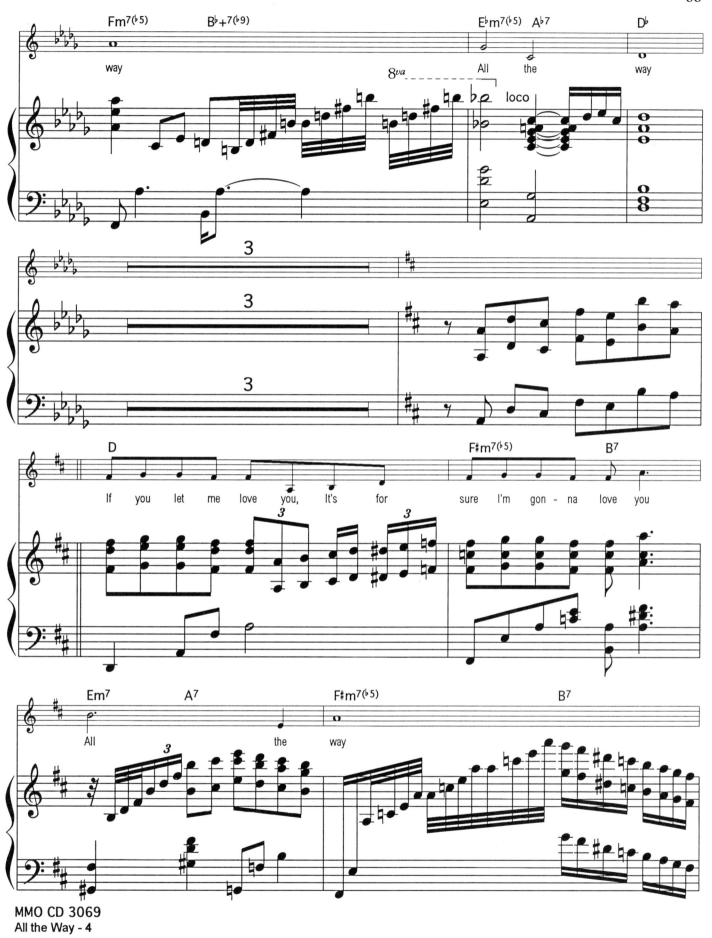

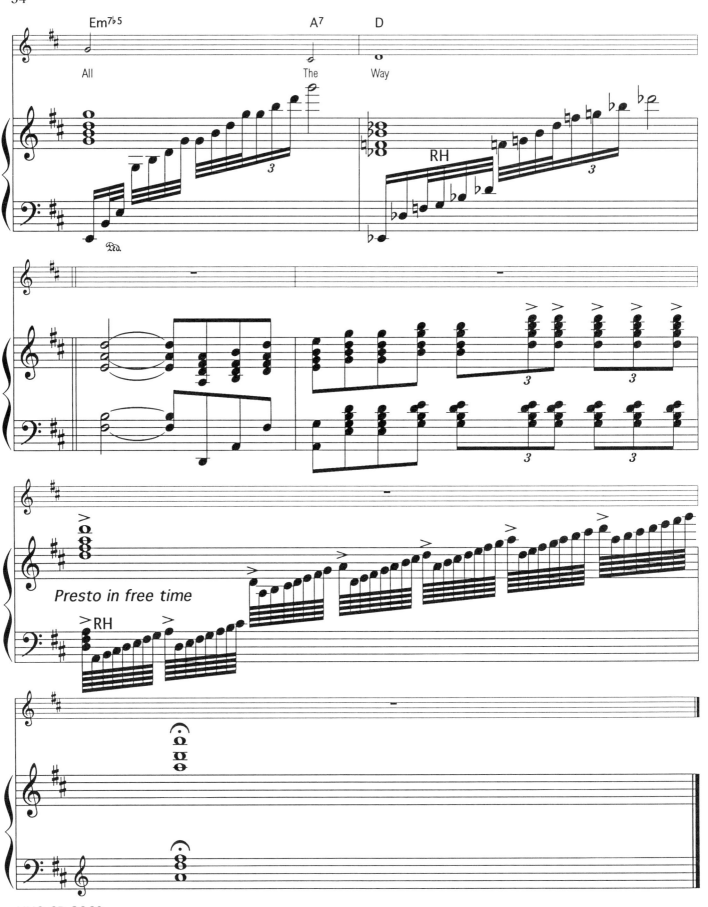

Piano

Brahms Concerto No.1 in D minor, Op.15 (2 CD Set) **MMO CD 3009**/344

Chopin Concerto No.1 in E minor, Opus 11 **MMO CD 3010**/343
This romantic concerto is one of the composer's few works with orchestra
and displays great lyricism and grandeur.

Mendelssohn Concerto No.1 in G minor,
Opus 25 **MMO CD 3011**/324

W. A. Mozart Concerto No.9 in Ebm, K.271 **MMO CD 3012**/328

W. A. Mozart Concerto No.12 in A, K.414 **MMO CD 3013**/351

W. A. Mozart Concerto No.20 in D minor, K.466 **MMO CD 3014**/308

W. A. Mozart Concerto No.23 in A, K.488 **MMO CD 3015**/323

W. A. Mozart Concerto No.24 in C minor, K.491 **MMO CD 3016**/335

W. A. Mozart Concerto No. 26 in D,
K.537,"Coronation" **MMO CD 3017**/309

W. A. Mozart Concerto No.17 in G, K.453 **MMO CD 3018**/352

Liszt Concerto No.1/ Weber Concertstucke **MMO CD 3019**/303

Liszt Concerto No. 2 in A/Hungarian Fantasia **MMO CD 3020/345**
The Hungarian Fantasia, with its triumphal themes, sparkling cadenzas, and
breathtaking finale is a gem.

J.S. Bach Concerto in F Minor
J.C. Bach Concerto in Eb **MMO CD 3021/346**
Student concerti for the beginner, by father and son. J.C. Bach, the
youngest son of J.S. Bach, was also a skillful and prolific composer, as this
work will testify.

J.S. Bach Concerto in D Minor **MMO CD 3022**/317

Haydn Concerto in D major **MMO CD 3023**/311
A student level concerto, one of the most popular in the MMO Catalog.

Heart of the Piano Concerto **MMO CD 3024**/341
Great themes from the most famous piano concertos. Fun for all pianists!
Bach: Brandenberg No.5 (Allegro); Concerto In D (Adagio) (Allegro Moderato) **C.P.E. Bach:**
(Allegro Assai); **Haydn:** Concerto In D (Vivace, Allegro Assai) **Mozart:** Concerto In Eb K271
(Allegro) Concerto In D Minor K466 (Romance) (Allegro); K488 (Allegro) (Allegro Assai);
K491(Larghetto); K537 (Allegro) **Beethoven:** Concerto No.1. (Largo); No.2 (Allegro Con Brio)
(Adagio); Op.37(Allegro Con Brio); Op. 58 (Allegro Moderato) Op.73 (Adagio un poco moto)
(Rondo-Allegro) **Mendelssohn;** Concerto No.1 In G (Molto Allegro) (Andante); Schumann:
Concerto In A minor (Allegro Affettuoso) **Liszt:** Concerto No.1 (Allegro Maestoso)
Tchalkovsky: Concerto No.1 (Allegro Non Troppo); Concerto No.2 (Andantino)
Rachmaninoff: Concerto No.2 (Moderato) **Grelg:** (Adagio) Excerpts from the movements
indicated are played.

Beethoven Concerto No.1 in C, Opus 15 **MMO CD 3001**/314

Beethoven Concerto No. 2 in Bb, Opus 19 **MMO CD 3002**/316

Beethoven Concerto No.3 in C minor, Op.37 **MMO CD 3003**/315

Beethoven Concerto No.4 in G, Opus 58 **MMO CD 3004**/336

Beethoven Concerto No.5 in Eb, Opus 73 (2 CD Set) **MMO CD 3005**/334
The five great piano concerti! In these works, Beethoven enlarged and
intensified the breadth and scope of the classical form. Between the first
and fifth piano concerto, the development of his style and his particular
innovations are evident.
The spirited, graceful, wonderfully pianistic Concerto No. 1 in C, written
actually after the second concerto, the Mozartian Concerto No. 2 in Bb
major, and the Concerto No. 3 in C minor with its striking passages, were
written for and performed on a forerunner of the modern piano, lighter in
tone and restricted in dynamic range. The introspective yet lofty Concerto
No. 4 in G major, not popular until Mendelssohn revived it in 1836, thirty
years after it was composed, and the mighty ever-popular Concerto No. 5
in Eb major, named "Emperor" by an unidentified publisher, had the
advantage of the more modern piano.

Grieg Concerto in A minor, Op.16 **MMO CD 3006**/312
One of the most popular offerings in the MMO catalogue. It is less
demanding and accessible to the serious student.

Rachmaninoff Concerto No. 2 in C minor **MMO CD 3007**/333
Equally renowned as composer and pianist, Rachmaninoff dazzled the
world with his piano concerto in C minor. It is immensely popular to this
day. Brilliant and powerful with the beautiful lyric theme that became the
popular song Full Moon and Empty Arms, it is here presented in a lovely
recording, sans your part, the solo piano.

Schumann Concerto in A minor, Op.54 **MMO CD 3008**/326
A favorite in piano literature, the concerto embodies the melodic grace and
fine tonal textures so characteristic of the composer.

Teach Me Tonight

The intro is smooth and lilting. Piano starts with straight-forward melody in octaves supported by LH chords. The piano then begins improvising around the melody with the faintest trace of "Errol Garnerisms" (Garner made the original definitive recording of this song). The bridge utilizes the varied textures offered by broken octaves, single note with LH chords, and block chords. The rest of the piece proceeds in similar fashion with stylistic pianisms, the piano playing figures with the band, and occasional subtle references to the ever-ebullient Garner. If you have not already done so, you should treat yourself to some of his wonderful recordings. J. O.

Words by Sammy Cahn
Music by Gene De Paul

MMO CD 3069
Teach Me Tonight - 1

58

Teach Me Tonight - 3

62

MMO CD 3069

Teach Me Tonight - 7

FOR PIANISTS

I've Got You Under My Skin
It Might As Well Be Spring
Come Rain Or Come Shine
Witchcraft
Young At Heart
It's All Right With Me
This is All I Ask
The Best Is Yet To Come
All The Way
Teach Me Tonight

3069

MUSIC MINUS ONE 50 Executive Boulevard • Elmsford New York 10523-1325